THE GOSPEL OF ISAIAH

Philip Holdway-Davis

THE GOSPEL OF ISAIAH

Publisher
Insurance Professional Limited

Copyright © 2021
Philip Holdway-Davis

PO Box 11-603
Ellerslie
Auckland 1542
New Zealand

www.thesoulsong.co.nz
Created by: Philip Holdway-Davis

Copyright quotation rights:
Commercial Use
You must receive permission from Philip Holdway-Davis

Private, Personal & Not-for-Profit Use
This book is free to use for personal and not-for-profit use. Also freely use it for reprinting, quoting and public speaking. The words "used with the permission of Philip Holdway-Davis www.thesoulsong.co.nz" must appear at the end of the quotation(s).

ISBN 978-0-473-53206-2 (Softcover)
ISBN 978-0-473-53207-9 (Epub)

Printed in New Zealand

Contents

Introduction 1

The Prayer of Jesus 3

The SoUL Song 4

Introduction to: The Gospel of Isaiah 10

Prophecy Table 12

THE GOSPEL OF ISAIAH 17

The Good Confession 22

Introduction

This *Written Miracle* is an ancient prophecy and prediction concerning the appearing of *The Christ*. This prophecy was made hundreds of years before Christ appeared. It was miraculously fulfilled with pin-point accuracy by Jesus of Bethlehem and Nazareth. These prophecies and predictions belong alongside a large number of prophecies from the Holy Bible's Old Testament. There are so many of them (you can see a few of them in the Gospel of Isaiah and the Prophecy Table further on) that they could only have been put there by Holy Spirit. Certain Jewish scholars, who did not want Jesus to be their Messiah or Christ, started deleting a few of the more obvious prophecies, but it appears there were too many, so they gave up or were stopped. As these are Holy Spirit Words, when you read, hear, touch or speak them you are engaging with GOD because you are reading, hearing, touching and speaking EHYER (EHYER is the Name that GOD revealed to Moses in Exodus 3:14). GOD and EHYER's Word, Holy Spirit, GOD's Name and Unconditional Love are all one and the same. As these prophesy words are miraculous, it is logical and reasonable to keep applying these miracle words for healing of the heart, spirit, mind, and body – in fact, to anything organic whether animal or plant. Why not try it and see?

Whilst this miracle Gospel is short in length, it is full of GOD's power and potency. These supernatural Words are worth more than pure gold. Everything of value according to this world will rot and disappear, but the Words in *The Gospel of Isaiah* will never pass away but will remain with us forever (Luke 21:33).

The Gospel of Isaiah belongs to a collection of thirty books called *Scriptures of Unconditional Love*. There are the books of written miracles being the *Four-Gospels-In-Advance*, the twenty-two books of *EHYER's Witnesses* and four books of *Enlightenment*. All these books are or will be FREE to download from www.thesoulsong.co.nz or can be purchased online as an e-book or in hard copy which you can receive by post mail.

I have added various components such as *The Prayer of Jesus* (The LORD's Prayer), *Introduction to: The Gospel of Isaiah, The Good Confession and The SoUL Song*, in case you wanted to use *The Gospel of Isaiah* as the central core of a worship activity. Worship EHYER either on your own (Matthew 6:6) or with other people. Start with reciting "Draw near to GOD and EHYER will come close to you" (James 4:8.), then go from there. Don't be too rigid or legalistic but be flexible and open to GOD inspiration as you might be touched to include or exclude Holy Spirit stuff as EHYER moves in your heart. You might be alone or isolated, but if you humbly recite these words you will draw close to GOD who will respond by coming close to you. Keep in touch with EHYER and GOD will never leave you or forsake you (Hebrews 13:5). You will never be alone ever again.

•

The Prayer of Jesus

Come near and draw close to GOD and GOD will draw near to you
– James 4:8

The Spirit of Jesus is EHYER ASHER EHYER which is the Name GOD told Moses when asked (Exodus 3:14).

EHYER told us to pray these words of GOD:
"Our Father in Heaven,
May your Name be kept Holy,
Your Kingdom come,
Your Will be done on earth as it is in heaven.
Give us enough bread to eat today.
Forgive us our sin as we have forgiven those who have sinned against us.
Do not allow us to be tempted, but deliver us from the Evil One.
Yours is the power and the glory forever and ever."

- *The Witness of The Twelve Apostles.*

The SoUL Song

https://youtu.be/bS2d0-Skpzc

Insert the above address into your browser to see and hear *The SoUL Song.*

These are the words to *The SoUL Song* which is short for *The Scriptures of Unconditional Love Song*. It's a song that glorifies GOD's Name and is full of Holy Spirit. It is not copyrighted for personal or not-for-profit use, so you can use it wherever and whenever you like providing there is no change to the Words. I would love to one day hear that it is being sung in classical, heavy metal, jazz, Chinese traditional, salsa and in every genre and in every language.

EHYER ASHER EHYER (GOD's original Name in Exodus 3:14 in Hebrew)
IHU KARAITI (Jesus Christ in Maori)
EGO SUM QUI SUM (GOD's Name in Exodus 3:14 in Latin)
I AM WHO AM (GOD's Name in Exodus 3:14 in English)

EHYER ASHER EHYER
I AM THE WAY (John 14:6)
I AM THE TRUTH (John 14:6)
I AM THE LIFE (John 14:6)

EHYER ASHER EHYER
IHU KARAITI
EGO SUM QUI SUM
I AM WHO AM

EHYER ASHER EHYER
I AM THE LIGHT (John 8:12)
I AM THE DOOR (John 10:9)
I AM THE GOOD (John 10:11)

EHYER ASHER EHYER
IHU KARAITI
EGO SUM QUI SUM
I AM WHO AM

EHYER ASHER EHYER
I AM THE SHEPHERD (John 10:11)
I AM THE BREAD (John 6:35)
I AM THE VINE (John 15:5)

EHYER ASHER EHYER
IHU KARAITI
EGO SUM QUI SUM
I AM WHO AM

EHYER ASHER EHYER
I AM THE RESURRECTION (John 11:25)
I AM THE START (Revelation 1:17)
I AM THE END (Revelation 2:8)

EHYER ASHER EHYER
IHU KARAITI
EGO SUM QUI SUM
I AM WHO AM

EHYER ASHER EHYER
I AM THE ALPHA (Revelation 1:8)
I AM THE OMEGA (Revelation 22:13)
I AM WHO AM

EHYER ASHER EHYER
Baptise me with Your Spirit (Matthew 3:11)
In the Name of the Father (Matthew 28:19)
Son & Holy Spirit (Matthew 28:19)

EHYER ASHER EHYER
IHU KARAITI
EGO SUM QUI SUM
I AM WHO AM

EHYER ASHER EHYER
IHU KARAITI REPUTE (Reputation of the Name of Ihu Karaiti or Jesus Christ)
Heal my heart and spirit (Psalm 51:10)
Heal my body and mind (Exodus 15:26 & 23: 25)

EHYER ASHER EHYER
IHU KARAITI
EGO SUM QUI SUM
I AM WHO AM

EHYER ASHER EHYER

GOD gave to Moses GOD's Name. In Exodus 3:14, GOD says GOD's Name is EHYER ASHER EHYER. In the 4th century, it was translated from Hebrew into Latin by the renowned Jewish scholar Jerome as EGO SUM QUI SUM. In English it translates as I AM WHO AM.

> **Latin:** Dixit Deus ad Mosen EGO SUM QUI SUM ait sic dices filiis Israhel qui est misit me ad vos.
>
> **English:** God said to Moses: I AM WHO AM. He said: Therefore, you will say to the children of Israel: HE WHO IS, has sent me to you.

The Name EHYER ASHER EHYER may confuse a number of people who thought the Name was Jehovah or Yahweh or something else instead. In fact, in Exodus 3:15 GOD tells Moses to say that GOD's Name is YHVH (YUD-HEH-VAV-HEH). Unfortunately, ancient scholars deleted the vowels long ago and just left us with the consonants, so people have had to guess the spelling and so they came up with Jehovah and Yahweh etc. EHYER = I AM. YHVH = HE IS. One is first person the other third person.

    Moses was GOD's friend who talked face to face with GOD. Moses was the humblest person on earth (Numbers 12:3). GOD even shared with Moses what GOD was like as a person: *"I am the LORD God. I am merciful and compassionate. I show great love, and I can be trusted."* – Exodus 34:6

The people of Israel at that time were hard-hearted. After seeing many miracles whilst being set free from slavery in Egypt, they made a golden calf and start worshipping it instead of GOD.

My position is that EHYER ASHER EHYER is GOD's Name for those who want to be in a relationship with GOD like Moses had. YHVH-Jehovah-Yahweh is for those who recognise and appreciate GOD but prefer to keep a little distance. Either way, both Names can be called upon and GOD can be engaged with.

IHU KARAITI

Ihu Karaiti is Maori for Yahshua Messiah (Hebrew) or Jesus Christ (English). I believe, as many scholars do, that it was the Spirit of Ihu or Jesus who spoke to Moses from the burning bush. Ihu Karaiti represents the indigenous peoples' Name for Yahshua Messiah. I would like it also to represent the pre-colonial, pre-crusade and pre-church eras to reach out to everyone in the whole world.

I AM

I emphasise *I AM* because it's a Name Jesus called himself just as GOD did 1,500 years prior. Some scholars, including myself, are convinced that EHYER ASHER EHYER is, in fact, the Spirit of Jesus, or the Spirit of Christ, or the Son of GOD, talking to Moses from the burning bush in Exodus 3. Jesus says I AM on a number of occasions. In the Book of John, we read that the religious leaders picked up stones to kill Jesus when Jesus said, "I AM" (John 8:59 & John 10:30-33).

There are so many similarities between the events concerning Exodus and Jesus of Bethlehem and Nazareth that can only be explained as miracle intervention by GOD.

Introduction To: The Gospel of Isaiah

Isaiah ended up being sawn in two inside a log. But not before he had succeeded in delivering GOD's messages to us. He became one of the famous major Prophets. These prophecies are taken from the Book of Isaiah and mainly from Chapter 53. They were written about 600 years before Christ appeared. They provide us with a clear picture that the Christ-Messiah must suffer. Christ suffering? Yes. Jesus the Christ had to truly suffer in order to destroy the works of Devil-Satan's death, decay and suffering so that we could be liberated from this existing hell. Hell? Hell yes! Whilst there may be pretty goings-on on nature's surface with all the birds, animals, trees, flowers, oceans etc., take a look closer and you will see a carnage of survival-of-the-fittest with rape, pillage, murder, pain and suffering at every level of life on earth.

Devil-Satan is the, now temporary, ruler of this world (John 14:30) but because of being out-manoeuvred by EHYER, the reign is fast coming to an end. It is logical to accept the fact that wherever Devil-Satan is, which right now is here on earth, there is hell. Some people choose not to believe in EHYER because of all the pain and suffering, but the truth is that all our pain and suffering is a consequence of the work of Devil-Satan.

The Good News Gospel is that Jesus has started to destroy and phase out all pain and all suffering. Even Devil-Satan's bone-cancerin-children is going to be destroyed by Jesus eventually and never seen, or heard of, again. Why not join in the fight, battles and war against Devil-Satan and start applying Holy Spirit written miracle words against every evil infliction? If you choose to accept this mission, you will be carrying out the work and Will of Jesus the Christ (1 John 3:8).

Some of the Jewish leaders, who murdered the Christ-Messiah, tried to delete prophesies from their Scriptures because they were too compelling as evidence that Jesus of Bethlehem and Nazareth was indeed the Christ-Messiah who was actually described centuries in advance. Whilst Isaiah 53 was never deleted entirely, eventually, it became forbidden to be read in most, if not all, synagogues. According to some scholars, the 17th-century Jewish historian, Raphael Levi, admitted that because Isaiah 53 caused "arguments and great confusion" the rabbis decided the best thing to do was to take the prophecy out of the Haftarah readings in the synagogues. They stop someway through Isaiah 52 and jump straight to Isaiah 54 instead. The official synagogue line today is that Isaiah 53's *Suffering Messiah* is a metaphor for the Jews who suffered at the hands of the non-Jews. This could be a plausible explanation, if this was the only prophecy, but it isn't. There are hundreds of them, many of which point to the suffering of the Messiah. The banning of Isaiah 53 is a symptom of a hard and uncircumcised heart. Read the *Gospel of Isaiah* amongst all the other prophecies yourself and make up your own mind.

Before you do, here is a taster of some of the typical prophecies and predictions included in the *Four Gospels-In-Advance:*

Prophecy Table

All dates are approximate in this table. Experts differ in their opinions, so I have taken the most likely dates. Ancient prophesies in the Holy Bible's Old Testament concerning the appearing of Christ, were used by the Original First Christians to prove that Jesus of Bethlehem and Nazareth was the Christ-Messiah. These prophecies were made hundreds, sometimes over a thousand years before Christ appeared yet they all accurately came true. There are many other prophecies that are not mentioned here.

Year	Event	Prophecy Made	Prophecy Fufilled
6 BC	The time had come for GOD to send his Son, born of a woman. Death had entered the world through Adam and now the first stage of God's plan to abolish death was being carried out.	Genesis 3:15	Galatians 4:4 Luke 2:7 Revelation 12:4–5
6 BC	Promised offspring of Abraham	Genesis 12:2–3	Matthew 1:1
		Genesis 18:18	Luke 3:34
			Acts 3:25
6 BC	Promised offspring of Isaac	Genesis 17:19	Matthew 1:2 Luke 3:34

Year	Event	Prophecy Made	Prophecy Fulfilled
6 BC	Promised offspring of Jacob	Genesis 28:14 Numbers 24:17	Matthew 1:2 Luke 3:34
6 BC	Descended from the tribe of Judah	Genesis 49:10	Matthew 1:2-16 Luke 3: 23-33
6 BC	From the family of David, the son of Jesse and heir to the throne of David	Psalm 132: 11 Isaiah 9:7	Matthew 1:1-16. Matthew 9:27 Acts 13:22-23
6 BC	Born in Bethlehem (probably around 25th September)	Micah 5:2	Matthew 2:1 Luke 2:4-11 John 7:42
6 BC	Born of a virgin	Isaiah 7:14	Matthew 1:18-23 Luke 1:30-35
6 BC	The Son of David	1 Chronicles 17:11-15	Matthew 22:41-42
6 BC	A prophet like Moses	Deuteronomy 18:18-19	John 5:45-47
4 BC	Murder of infants	Jeremiah 31:15	Matthew 2:16-18
4 BC	Escape into Egypt	Hosea 11:1	Matthew 2:14-15
AD 29	John the Baptist begins his ministry as "The Messenger"	Isaiah 40:3 Malachi 3:1	Matthew 3:1-3
AD 30	Anointed by the Spirit	Isaiah 42:1	Luke 3:21-22
AD 30	Jesus begins his commission	Isaiah 61:1-2	Luke 4:18-21
AD 30	Galilee sees a great light	Isaiah 9:1-2	Matthew 4:12-16
AD 30	Miracles	Isaiah 35:4-6	Matthew 11:2-6

Year	Event	Prophecy Made	Prophecy Fulfilled
AD 30	The Prophet	Deuteronomy 18:15	John 6:14 John 1:45 Acts 3:19-26
AD 30	Not believed	Isaiah 53:1–3	John 12:37-38 Romans 10:11&16
AD 30	Hated for no reason	Psalm 69:4	Luke 23:13-25 John 15:23-25
AD 33	Carried our sicknesses	Isaiah 53:4	Matthew 8:16-17
AD 33	Devoted enthusiasm for the house of GOD	Psalm 69:9	Matthew 21:12-13 John 2:13-17
AD 33	Triumphal entry into Jerusalem riding on the foal of a donkey	Zechariah 9:9	Matthew 21:6-9 John 12:12-16
AD 33	Hailed as King and one coming in the name of GOD	Psalm 118:26 Zechariah 9:9	Matthew 21:1-9 Mark 11:7-11
AD 33	Rejected by the Jews	Isaiah 53:3	John 1:11
AD 33	Rejected but becoming chief cornerstone	Psalm 118:22-23 Isaiah 28:16	Matthew 21:42-46 Acts 3:14 Acts 4:11 1 Peter 2:1-8
AD 33	Betrayed by one of his friends and disciples	Psalm 42:9 Psalm 109:8	Matthew 26:14-15 Matthew 26:47-50 Mark 14:10 John 13:18, 26-30
AD 33	Betrayed for 30 pieces of silver	Zechariah 11:12	Matthew 26:15 Matthew 27:3-15 Mark 14:10-11
AD 33	Money to be returned to buy a potter's field	Jeremiah 32:6-9 Zechariah 11:13	Matthew 27:6-7
AD 33	The betrayer's place taken by another	Psalm 69:25 Psalm 109:7-8	Acts 1:16-20

Year	Event	Prophecy Made	Prophecy Fulfilled
AD 33	Accused by false witnesses	Psalm 27:12	Matthew 26:60-61
AD 33	Tried and condemned	Isaiah 53:8	Matthew 26:57-68 Matthew 27:1-2 & 11-26
AD 33	Silent when accused	Isaiah 53:7	Matthew 26:62-63 Matthew 27:12-14 Mark 14:61 Mark 15:4-5
AD 33	Whipped and punched in the face	Isaiah 52:14 Isaiah 53:5	John 19:1-3
AD 33	Beaten and spat upon	Isaiah 50:6 Micah 5:1	Matthew 26:67 Matthew 27:26&30 Mark 14:65 John 19:3
AD 33	Mocked and insulted	Psalm 22:6-8	Matthew 27:39-40
AD 33	Mocked by prophetic words	Psalm 22:8	Matthew 27:39-40
AD 33	Soldiers gamble for his clothing	Psalm 22:18	Matthew 27:35 John 19:23-24
AD 33	Crucified among sinners	Isaiah 53:12	Matthew 27:38 Luke 22:37
AD 33	Given vinegar and gall (wine vinegar mixed with bitter herbs to dull the pain)	Psalm 69:21	Matthew 27:34&48 Mark 15:23&36
AD 33	Forsaken by GOD	Psalm 22:1	Matthew 27:46 Mark 15:34
AD 33	No bones broken	Exodus 12:46 Psalm 34:20	John 19:33, 36
AD 33	Pierced through his hands and feet	Psalm 22:16 Zechariah 12:10	Luke 24:39-40 John 19:34-37 John 20:25-27 Revelation 1:7

Year	Event	Prophecy Made	Prophecy Fulfilled
AD 33	His side would be pierced	Zechariah 12;10	Matthew 27:49 John 19:34 John 20:25-27
AD 33	Sacrifices life to die and pay for our sins	Isaiah 53:5, 8, 11-12	Matthew 20:28 John 1:29 Romans 3:24 Romans 4:25
AD 33	Buried with the rich	Isaiah 53:9	Matthew 27:57-60 John 19:38-42
AD 33	His followers would desert him	Zechariah 13:7	Mark 14:27
AD 33	Dead for 3 days and nights then resurrected. The first stage of the abolition of death had been completed.	Hosea 6:2 Jonah 1:17 Jonah 2:10	Matthew 12:39-40 Matthew 16:21 Matthew 17:23 Matthew 27:64 Luke 24:6-7
AD 33	Dead body did not decay	Psalm 16:10	Matthew 28:9 Luke 24:36-43
AD 33	Ascended into heaven	Psalm 68:18	Luke 24:50-51
AD 33	Sat down at the right hand of the Father	Psalm 110:1	Hebrews 1:2-3

THE GOSPEL OF ISAIAH

(Isaiah 50:6, 52:13-15, & Isaiah 53)

Prophecy Made: 580 BC

Prediction Fulfilled: AD 33 by Jesus of Bethlehem and Nazareth

THE PROPHECY

Look! My servant will act with wisdom. He will be highly placed, highly exalted, and highly elevated.

Many stared in amazement at his appearance, which was disfigured more than any man and his form marred beyond human likeness.

Likewise, he will startle many nations. Kings will be speechless in his presence, for they will see what they have not been told and understand what they have not heard.

Who has put their trust in our message? As for GOD's power, who has GOD revealed it to?

He will come up like a branch from a tree, like a root from dry land. He has no status or beauty that would cause us to consider him. There is nothing in his appearance that would make us desire him.

He was despised and people avoided him. He was a man destined for pain. He was surrounded by sicknesses. People turned their faces away from him, they considered him to be worth nothing.

He truly took upon himself our sicknesses and carried our pain, but we thought that he was cursed, that GOD had inflicted wounds on him and punished him.

He was pierced for our rebellion. He was crushed for our sins. He was punished so that we could obtain peace. Because of his wounds, we have been healed.

Like sheep, we have all strayed away. Every one of us has turned to go our own way, yet GOD has laid all of our sins on him.

He was abused and allowed himself to receive punishment, but he did not protest against it. He was brought like a lamb to the slaughter. He was like a sheep that is silent when being sheared. He would not open his mouth. He was arrested, taken away and judged.

"I gave my back to the strikers, and my cheeks to those pulling out my beard; I turned and faced their insults and spitting."

Who would have thought that he would be put to death? He was killed because of the sin of my people.

He was buried in a tomb alongside the wicked and the rich were there too in his death, even though he had done nothing violent and had never spoken a lie.

GOD himself was pleased to crush him and willing to make him suffer. GOD made his life a sacrifice for all the wrong we have all done, and because of that, he will have offspring for many days. Through his pleasing work, GOD's Will has been achieved.

He will see, understand, and become completely satisfied because of his pain. My righteous servant will save many people because he has taken on their sins. He has righteous knowledge through what he has learned.

Therefore, I will give him a share among the mighty. He will divide this prize with many, due to the fact he poured out his life in death and he was counted as if he was a sinner. He carried the sins of many people and now intercedes for the rebellious.

PREDICTION FULFILMENT
(Matthew, Mark, Luke & John)

Jesus was taken away to the high priest. All the chief priests, leaders and scribes joined to visit him. The whole council along with the chief priests tried to find people to witness against Jesus, so they could kill him, but could not find anyone. Some gave false testimonies about Jesus, but the testimonies conflicted with each other.

Some false witnesses arose and said, *"He said, 'I will destroy this temple built by hand, and in three days' time I will build another one made without hands.'"* Even then, their testimonies conflicted with each other. The high priest arose amongst them, and asked Jesus, *"Have you nothing to say to answer them? What exactly are they accusing you of?"* But he remained silent and did not answer them. Again, the high priest questioned him, *"Are you the Christ, the Son of GOD?"* Jesus said, *"I am. You will look at the Son of Man placed at the right hand of power and coming upon the clouds in the sky."* The high priest ripped his clothing, saying, *"Why do we need any more witnesses? You have heard him blaspheme! Do you agree?"* Every one of them condemned him to deserve death. A few began to spit on him, cover his face and start punching him. They said, *"Prophesy!"* and the officers slapped him using the palms of their hands.

As soon as it was morning, the chief priests, leaders, scribes, and the whole council, had a meeting. They tied Jesus up, and took him away to be given to Pilate. Pilate questioned him, *"Are you the King of the Jews?"* He answered, *"So you say."* The chief priests accused him on a number of matters. Pilate again questioned him, *"Don't you have an answer? Can you see all the matters they accuse you of?"* But Jesus remained silent. Pilate marvelled at this. Pilate questioned the crowd again, *"What then should I do to him whom you call the King of the Jews?"* They again shouted out, *"Crucify him!"* Pilate replied, *"Why, what wrong has he committed?"* But they cried out even louder, *"Crucify him!"* Pilate, wanting to make the crowd happy, released Barabbas. He then handed over Jesus to be flogged and sent him away to be crucified.

The soldiers led him away inside the court that is known as the Praetorium. Then they summoned the entire cohort. They dressed him up in purple, and after weaving together a crown of thorns, they placed it on his head. They started to salute him and say, *"Hail the King of the Jews!"* They reed-swiped his head, spat on him, then bowing down upon their knees, pretended to worship him. After they had their laugh at his expense, they snatched back the purple robe and dressed him in his own clothing. Then they took him away to crucify him.

In the evening after he had died, along came a rich man from Arimathea called Joseph, who was also a disciple of Jesus. Joseph approached Pilate to request that he give Jesus's body to him. Pilate commanded that the body was to be handed over. Joseph took the body, wrapped it in a clean linen cloth, placed it in his own new tomb (which he had cut out of the rock) then had a large stone rolled over to cover the entrance. Then he left.

On Sunday, very early in the morning, the women visited the tomb. They had prepared and brought spices. They arrived at the tomb but found the stone rolled away. When the women entered the tomb, they did not find the body of Jesus the Christ inside it. Whilst trying to work out what was going on here, two men dressed in radiant clothing came and stood next to them.

Whilst the women fell down and buried their faces into the ground out of sheer terror, they were asked the following question by the two men, *"Why look for people who are alive amongst those who have died? He is not here; He has risen! Remember what He told you when you were still in Galilee? 'The Son of Man has to be given into the control of sinful men, they will crucify him, then on the third day he will rise up from the dead.'"*

The Good Confession

The Good Confession is a composite statement about Jesus the Christ written by Ignatius of Antioch. He wrote it within 10 years of the death of the Apostle John. He was a friend of Polycarp, a disciple of the Apostle John, and apparently was appointed leader of the community of GOD's people in Antioch (Syria) by the Apostle Peter. This is the earliest and most accurate truth we have about who Jesus of Bethlehem and Nazareth really was. It's as if the Apostle John, the disciple who Jesus loved (John 21:7), was saying these truths through Ignatius himself. Ignatius was very close to the communities of EHYER's people in Philadelphia and Smyrna. These two communities were the only two out of seven that did not receive a rebuke from Jesus the Christ (Revelation 1-3):

We agree with the Apostles and believe that there is only one Healer who is made of both flesh and spirit, born and unborn, GOD in the flesh, true life surrounded by death, son of Mary and Son of GOD, initially experiencing suffering then afterwards beyond suffering – Jesus the Christ our RULER.

For our GOD, Jesus the Christ:

- ♥ Was conceived in Mary's womb according to the pre-planning of GOD and by the Holy Spirit

- ♥ Is physically descended from the line of David according to ancestry
- ♥ Is the Son of GOD according to the will and power of GOD
- ♥ Was born the son of Mary when she was still a virgin
- ♥ Ate and drank among us, both before being killed and after being raised up to life again
- ♥ Was baptised by John in order that all righteousness might be fulfilled by him
- ♥ Was nailed and crucified for us in his physical body under Pontius Pilate and Herod the Tetrarch
- ♥ Died in full sight of persons in heaven, on earth, and under the earth
- ♥ Was physically and spiritually raised from the dead when his Father raised him up
- ♥ Was touched and handled by his disciples after his resurrection. His disciples then saw that he was composed of flesh whilst being spiritually united with the Father at the same time. For this reason, his disciples also treated death with the same contempt.

He suffered all these things for our sakes so that we might be saved and likewise be raised up from the dead by the Father if we exercise trust in Jesus the Christ.

He has raised up a standard for all ages through his resurrection, to rally together his holy and faithful people whether among Jews or non-Jews, in the one body of the Community of GOD's people.

Other Books by Philip Holdway-Davis:

Triumph on the Western Front

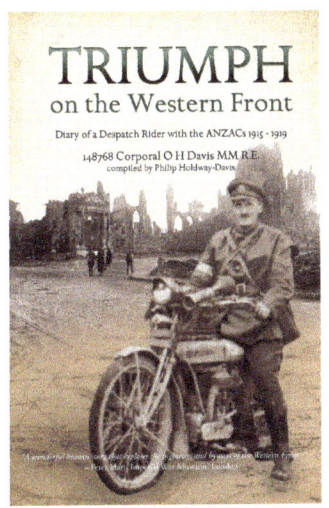

ISBN: 9-780473-314637

Share the experiences of a Despatch Rider during World War 1 by reading his own words written as a diary during his years on the Western Front. As an author of a dozen books, a journalist and a decent Christian Church of England man, Oswald writes descriptively and takes you on a journey through his eyes during WW1. He puts you on his trusty steed, his 1915 Triumph motorcycle, and dashes you around the battlefields of the Somme and Ypres.

Oswald Harcourt Davis joined the Royal Engineers in 1916 and arrived in Abbeville, Somme, France in July that year. He was attached to the ANZACs and dished out a Triumph motorcycle to carry pigeons and vital messages at a time when communications were limited and risky.

Read in fascinating detail his journeys around the Somme and Ypres Salient areas and the difficulties he had to face. Ever facing the danger of being "bumped" and "knocked" he rose to duty's call and made sure the pigeons got through. He cheated death on several occasions and admits he was scared and on the brink of cowardice, yet he was brave enough for decoration. He was awarded the Military Medal at Messines.

The book is available for free download or purchase by inserting the following address into your browser: www.triumphonthewesternfront.com.

www.ingramcontent.com/pod-product-compliance
Lightning Source LLC
Chambersburg PA
CBHW062029290426
44108CB00025B/2833